Senegal Taxi

Camino del Sol
A Latina and Latino Literary Series

Senegal Taxi

Juan Felipe Herrera

THE UNIVERSITY OF ARIZONA PRESS

www.uapress.arizona.edu

Library of Congress Cataloging-in-Publication Data
Herrera, Juan Felipe.
Senegal taxi : mud drawings / Juan Felipe Herrera.
p. cm. — (Camino del sol: a Latina and Latino literary series)
ISBN 978-0-8165-3015-1 (pbk. : acid-free paper)
I. Title.
PS3558.E74S46 2013
811'.54—dc23

                    2012028950

All royalties from the sales of this book will go to the cause of children in the new South Sudan.
Publication of this book is made possible in part by the proceeds of a permanent endowment
created with the assistance of a Challenge Grant from the National Endowment for the Humanities,
a federal agency.

Manufactured in the United States of America on acid-free, archival-quality paper containing a
minimum of 30% post-consumer waste and processed chlorine free.

18   17   16   15   14   13   6   5   4   3   2   1

For Ibrahim, Abdullah, Sahel

To the peoples of Darfur, of Africa, please forgive my limitations, this is a small offering.
To my father, Felipe Emilio, and mother, Lucha, migrant laborers, who taught me the art of kindness, sacrifice for others, story, and friendship.

To Marga Robles, my seer.
To my teachers, mentors, and friends, Renato Rosaldo, Tom Lutz, Michael Jayme, Marvin Bell, Gerald Stern, Phil Levine, and Elly Simmons.
To my editor, Kristen Buckles, and all the good people at the University of Arizona Press.
Many bows to a great hermano and thinker, Victor Martinez, and to a most dear and visionary human being, Nancy Hatamiya, RIP.
For my students.
For unity and peace.

After the bombings, we came and dug many graves . . . we cut wood from the trees to dig . . . after we buried them, we left.

—*Darfurian young man, about sixteen years old*

i made it up
here on this bridge between
starshine and clay
my one hand holding tight
my other hand; come celebrate
with me that everyday
something has tried to kill me
and has failed.

—*Lucille Clifton, "song at midnight,"* **Book of Light**

Acknowledgments

Kind acknowledgments to the Montalvo Arts Center in Saratoga, California, for an artist residency where an early version of this manuscript was drafted in 2009, and a bow to the resident artists who performed the initial sketch. Abundant gratitude to the John Simon Guggenheim Memorial Foundation for a poetry fellowship in 2010–11 allowing me to rethink and expand the text into its present form.

Senegal Taxi

Voices

1

In the gnashing sandstorm nights and in the days after the burials, in between the vagaries of escape and tattered voices of Darfur, massacred and burned, ambled three ghost children.

August 2004

Cave

On the mud walls of the cave where they hid, Ibrahim drew many things that happened to him and his village, he pushed out the shapes of the voices, the explosions of the Russian Antonov, the attacks and the burnings, the faces and the running blood. Gnarled flies and charred ants, the swarming jaws of the Kalashnikov AK-47, they echoed in that hole. Even the Janjaweed's crazy televison talk. How he rode with his men in search of Ibrahim and his brother and sister, his little band. When Janjaweed was lost and mad, he sat near the cave without knowing it. He directed a television game with his guards. Then he laughed long, waving the Kalash in the air.

Of the village, Ibrahim and his band were the only ones left—Abdullah, who always poked his one good eye, sang and spat out words here and there like bullets, Sahel, the youngest, who constructed tiny schools with sticks and the wings of dead beetles, and Ibrahim, son of Muhammad and Nasra, grandson of Um and Yaccoub. Wait, Ibrahim said. I see my mother ahead, guiding us. She carries a hungry child wrapped around her back. This is how she carried me and you—and you. It is a mirage. It is a cloud of ash sent to us from the ancestors who live at the foot of the mountains of Shugakaro. Ibrahim said. We must follow her footsteps to Senegal. Perhaps from there we will reach you. Ibrahim turned to the brown-black wall and smoothed his fingers on the spit-moist earth. I wish I could find the words to tell you the story of our village after you were killed. After we buried the ones we could find, he said to his mother and moved on with Sahel trailing after Abdullah.

The Village

Mud Drawing #1. The Village Ant

Wake up! Wake up! Wake up!

Wakeupwakeupwakeupwakeupwakeup!

Mud Drawing #2. The Antonov Bomb

Here I go
        Down below
                Here I go
                        Down below

                                            Who sent me?
                                  I don't know
                        Here I go

            Down below

Mud Drawing #3. The Kalashnikov AK-47

Came down the mountain
Saw them grazing cows by the mud wall
Noticed my father Antonov burning off their clothes
Came down the mountain and stumbled
On the gravestones of Shugakaro where the grandmothers lay
Before my father met them out in the open
The women dragged their children into a cave
I do not know why the others were hiding
In a circle around the split tree of the village
Came down the mountain as the sun broke

Mud Drawing #4. Sahel, the Village Girl

Wait for me   Abdullah!

I am kneeling down. Lifting a school
With leaves

Raise a classroom with sticks
Clean the chalkboard with wind
Set the table with mud
Write these letters with my forehead
Learn all there is to know in the world

Mud Drawing #5. The Village Fly

Janjaweed say Bat her down! Bat her down!
They think they have struck gold
They pause and pretend to examine me
They are not the patient kind, I must say. They idle
Their hands pulling their net bag steady
Or their muddy sandals or their Kalash in position
I know their game
They do not dare strike me. They will not risk
Having the Kalash break into its 24 moving faces
The camel killer, the Janjaweed, prides himself
On cleanliness. On order, if I may use that term
While I consider a pile of dung. But, Janjaweed
Does not study. That, comrade, is where I come in.

Mud Drawing #6. Ibrahim, the Village Boy

Gold.
That's what Mr. America wanted.

And his Janjaweed brothers. The ones herding us like camels, the ones shooting at us from their flying horses, the ones that rode through my village in Darfur. It was the gold that pulled me out of the cave. Where would a young man grab gold, you ask? How could a boy without a mother or a father or a grandmother, a boy with no one left in the village except one brother and one sister grab the gold?

My mother, Nasra, was hauled away by the Janjaweed. Hurt 100 times in ways I cannot mention. She died with her eyes open. That's when my father Muhammad left us in charge of our grandmother Um. So many things I learn inside this taxi, Ms. You tell me your story. I tell you story too. That's what a taxi man does, right? We tell story. We hear story. We make story.

Antonov! Ibrahim called. Antonov! But he couldn't stop the song from blowing out of Antonov's jaws into ten thousand tongues. All he could see from afar was the one-eye. When he shut his own eyes, the one-eye was still there. No matter how far Ibrahim and his brother Abdullah and his sister Sahel ran—the Antonov one-eye wheels glittered and raged over the lands.

On occasion in the vestiges of the last village hut an odd beige television box lay on its side crackling speaking somehow speaking as if it could still speak askew on the mud floor.

Television Box in the Last Village Hut

Juba, South Sudan, Africa

Inside the New Africa Series:

News Anchor Bart Crimson Interviews an Ex-Janjaweed

Confidential

Bart Crimson: This is your host, Bart Crimson, on your Bamba-K Channel. First of all, thanks for meeting with us, uh, Mr. Janjaweed. Is it ok to call you this? Well, ok . . . ah, let me start by asking you, Why are you here?

Janjaweed: Uh, ahh . . . Well . . .

Bart: Ah, come on! I mean after serving with Janjaweed, a paramilitary organization in many ways under the auspices of the old Sudanese government, by all accounts responsible for countless atrocities committed against the hundreds of thousands of villagers in Darfur and elsewhere, you know?

Janjaweed: Ahh, ahh . . . Yes . . . heh.

Bart: I mean, the numbers just boggle the mind. Oh, by the way, I must tell everyone that we are scrambling your voice and that we are only showing your silhouette. In addition to the mask, yes, yes. Well, alright, let's get to the question, we only have a half hour for this breaking news series—Why are you here?

Janjaweed: Heh, ahh, well. This is confusing. Well, these are my people. My Sudan. Not Sudan rebel dung.

Bart: Well, aren't you just a bandit with a government stamp? So . . . the difference being. . . ?

Janjaweed: I fight. For my Sudan. Like Sudan Army. Not like here. Where everybody has a pillow.

Bart: What? A pillow? Did you say, Pillow? Excuse me?

Janjaweed: A couch. A bed. A sofa, a pair curtains, a table, a plate, a spoon, and a glass of clean water.

Every time I pick up the Kalashnikov and ride into a village with fire I am fighting for one of these things. Don't see people falling. A pillow, I see it rising. A bed, maybe. Water. That is why I follow orders. That is all. But, there came. A limit. Heh.

Bart: Now there's a limit! What limit?

Janjaweed: I had a dream of a boy whose body was blown to bits.

Bart: And. . . ?

Janjaweed: Well, heh. Saw him from above. Hit by a flying burning stone. A stone. On fire. Up the sky he was flying. Then boom! Landed! Next to my feet looking up with his chest blown yellow eyes wrinkled face open eyes he had an old woman face and a hole big big hole on the right side of his chest all water leaking out I stood there looking down. And ahh.

Mud Drawing #7. The Village Ant

& leg muscle & hand scab &   eye sinew
& dust in groin & sweat   on nose
& green on nose & red   from nose
& tongue crawl &   bird-beak
& bird-eye rot & bee   head rot
& thorn in back & half-fly   on back
& wings float &   hairs burn
& tiny worm on baby head &   worm again
& lice on baby hand &   green again
& blue cloud on woman belly & blood   on black
& blood on dog & yellow skin   on bone

Mud Drawing #8. The Antonov Bomb

Children crumbling
      Children hiding
           Here I go
               Down below

                              With one eye
                        Made of ire
                                 Here I

go

           Down below

Mud Drawing #9. The Kalashnikov AK-47

Some refused to crawl
Some held a marriage ceremony later in the night and
Sang songs of lovers about to taste their flesh
Others formed a circle around them and hummed
And bowed their heads and churned their bodies
As if they were one
My father's open face of fire-flowers
Did not matter to them
I came down the mountain in full gallop
With my sister Mortar
And many brothers of the Kalash

Mud Drawing #10. Sahel, the Village Girl

I am spelling   Africa
I am spelling
Sudan
I am spelling
Darfur
I am spelling
Janjaweed
I am spelling the name of the president of Sudan

        Omar
                Hassan
                        Ahmad al-Bashir

Mud Drawing #11. Ibrahim, the Village Boy

I live in the Brooklyn now.

Facing Ibrahim. Janjaweed stood. His killing was done. When Ibrahim looked up he knew then that the killing was just beginning even though his village was shattered and smoldering. Everyone had been cut down by the Kalash. Even if the barrel was empty the killer still loved to hear it crackle and admired his touch on the target. Kill what next? Ibrahim said.

The television box threaded to the mud wall of the last scarred village hut somehow pulsed out of the earth the swirling voices.

Television Box in the Last Village Hut
Juba, South Sudan, Africa

Inside the New Africa Series:
News Anchor Bart Crimson Interviews an Ex-Janjaweed
Confidential

Janjaweed: Sometimes we killed ah, heh, everyone. In
the village. No one could tell who killed who. We
killed them all. Or we took women. Each one took one.
Where no one and everyone can see her. There. Heh.
Bart Crimson: Ugh . . . ahh. Well, let's talk about
the Russian Antonov planes. Before you went into the
village wasn't there already an airstrike, bombs?

Mud Drawing #12. Ibrahim, the Village Boy

Taxi! Taxi! People call. In the Brooklyn. Where? Senegal! I tell them. I
come from Senegal! No one knows Darfur. Sometimes I could drive-drive
back to my village. Father Muhammad herds cattle. Waves his hand so
I can help him. Mother Nasra plants sorghum. She is telling story with
the women. Little Sahel swats flies. Laughs when she hits one and it spins
dizzy to the earth. Stunned then dead. That was before Janjaweed.

Before genocide wars, father would say.
You said 2nd and Houston. In the village, right?

Mud Drawing #13. Sahel, the Village Girl

I am learning numbers you taught me   Abdullah!
Wait for me!   Wait, I said!

200,000 fled to Chad
Refugees   Abdullah!
200,000 dead. 200,000

2,000,000 left in fires and dust   Abdullah!
2,000,000

                                                          Abdullah?

Like us

Mud Drawing #14. Ibrahim, the Village Boy

Redsky Hotel. Good choice, Ms.
Tourists love Redsky. The Village. Makes me laugh a little. The way you
people say *The Village* here. I will tell you about my village. And how I
escaped by melting gold for Mr. America.

Of course. It wasn't gold metal.

Better than gold. Gold from the bowels of the Kalash the Janjaweed wrap
around their breast, horses, and camels. Kalashnikov gold. Most deadly.
Most precious!

Television Box in the Last Village Hut
Juba, South Sudan, Africa

Inside the New Africa Series:
News Anchor Bart Crimson Interviews an Ex-Janjaweed
Confidential

Bart Crimson: Yes. Go on please . . . go!
Janjaweed: Heh. Ahh. I couldn't stop the water. A piece of the boy's flesh in the shape of bread was to my left heh. Facing me. Not moving. But the boy was looking up at me with one yellow eye. A woman eye. When we ride into a village all of us shoot crazy at the same time until the Kalash burns in our hands. Until the dust and the screams return to dirt. Then all you hear is the whip of the winds. I follow order to kill the rebels. Do you know that? Rebel dung! Then I go to sleep. But after this dream I can't close my eyes. That is all I can tell you. Ahh. Heh.
Bart: I see I see . . . when you go on a raid how many Janjaweed go with you?

Janjaweed: Go with others. Like my brothers heh. Maybe twenty maybe more. We kill rebels against Sudan! You understand?

Bart: But you said you also kill children and women. Will you confirm that?

Mud Drawing #15. Abdullah, the Village Boy with One Eye

No village.

No mother. No father. One brother. One sister. No food. No water. No cows. No camels. No trees. No village. No food no water. No cows no camels no trees. No father no. Mother. No. One brother. One sister no water. No. One brother no water no father. No camel no cow no village no. No trees. No trees. No trees. No village no father. No mother no mother no mother. No water. No water. No. No village one sister. No mother. No water. One sister. One sister. One sister. No village. One sister. No village no trees no trees no father no. No mother. No camels no camels no village no trees no trees. No trees. One sister. One. Sister. One. No. Father. No father no food no food no food. No mother no mother. Onesister. No village no village no village. No village no village no village no village no trees.

They whipped their horses down the mountain as if they had erupted from the heart of Africa. As if Africa itself had sent the Janjaweed to hunt down Ibrahim, Abdullah, and Sahel. But, they were Africa. So, they stood there.

Mud Drawing #16. Ibrahim, the Village Boy

That's not all.
I will tell you how I hammered that gold into magic.

How I turned it into something like this orange-colored Taxi. Kalash gold.
Sewn with sun-brushed metals and hair-like thorns and voices slipping
out from the graveyards and beyond the road to Senegal beyond the blind
shores of Dakar.

Only one. One. One!
One person in the universe would be granted the journey. Could drive it
across Sudan across on the windstorms all the way here. The Brooklyn.
And that person Ms. was me. I bow down to my grandmother's spirit. Her
blessings. Mother Nasra's daily prayers. My father Muhammad's secret
army. It is all because of them.

The gold? I will tell you.

Mud Drawing #17. The Kalashnikov AK-47

After the ashes cleared I fell
By the stumps of flesh
I heard their whispers and furies I
Could not stop listening and peering into them
As my master slept

The television box spoke as if the ooze of the village faces and things and bodies and trees and eye-waters and sinews and more sands razor-slanting across the desert electrified it without mercy as the rebel father's children Ibrahim and Sahel and Abdullah and the villagers had been electrified with weapon fire without mercy electrified into ghosts by the shoot waves of paramilitary Janjaweed by the ancient craze wars of men and all spirits against themselves.

Television Box in the Last Village Hut

Juba, South Sudan, Africa

Inside the New Africa Series:

News Anchor Bart Crimson Interviews an Ex-Janjaweed

Confidential

Bart Crimson: You mentioned the Antonov bombs. Is that all?

Janjaweed: The planes went ahead of us. And helicopters. Then we followed them. Heh. We opened the road. For the rest to follow.

Bart: I am curious, why would a dream bother a man like you? A well-trained Janjaweed. With all these reinforcements, come on!

Mud Drawing #18. Abdullah, the Village Boy with One Eye

No food.
No   food.
No food.
No food no food no food no food. One
Sister one sister one oneoneoneone one oneoneone
No water water water no. No water. No.
No cows.
No   trees.
No
Trees.

Mud Drawing #19. Ibrahim, the Village Boy

One of the Janjaweed he calls himself Mr. America. Shoot them all!
He called his men after we slipped into the cave. Slice that woman! Hit
the goats and the cows! And the camels! And that sheep! He said. He
coughed on me. Stop! I am Mr. America! He was not Mr. America. He
was Janjaweed. My father taught me. Mr. America's men were on horses
making rounds through the village. He was driving his Toyota pick-up
with three other guards. The Kalash tight on their chest. Then he mounted
the back of the truck. Pointed at me said, Grab that slave!

Mud Drawing #20. The Village Ant

& gut rot & wood rot & tree rot & tree bone
& tree crackling & toe in the pot
& rind on rib & rind on head
& sweat on rib & rind on dead
& sweat on pin & soil on ass
& fire on claw & stool on ass
& stool on breast & hind scab & hind rot
& branch blood & camel on yellow
& green on sister eye in black
& blood on brother eye the one in red
& aching & popping & crapping
& picking & digging & crackling

Nasra, my mother, Ibrahim said. I do not want to talk about her. Yet, I must mention her. He said. So you will not forget how she was taken. How she stood up. How she was beaten, raped. How she was ripped apart. Behind the tree.

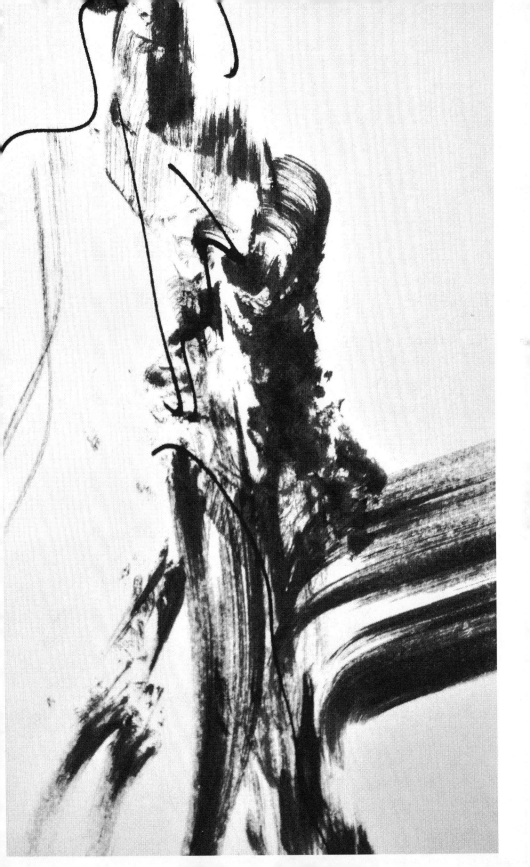

Mud Drawing #21. Sahel, the Village Girl

I am good at numbers
Dancing in front of me
Next to ancestor mountain
Count all my grandmothers
Pick up two handfuls of dust
This your dust?

I count the grandmothers then
They slip   I cannot find them   they
Become ash become one they become

                                                                    ash

Mud Drawing #22. The Village Fly

                                                Drift with elegance
Into the village burned or in a new formation.

My studies, comrade—
I am a student with a million eyes
Study dung
The ways and movement of cattle and goats
Study night soil
The bitter entrails and gases of the dead and the living.

Mud Drawing #23. Sahel, the Village Girl

I am making a school with leaves
I am learning all there is to know in the world
I am learning all there is to know in the world

Abdullah?

                              Abdullah!

Mud Drawing #24. Abdullah, the Village Boy with One Eye

All darkness in my eye even though the sun perches on a limb next to me webs of lights and the stars that I speak to drooling my arms ahead of me. Where? They ask me in starry breath pieces. Why are you running child? They say. Why through this smooth wind under the moon? I tell them that I cannot see that I can barely breathe that all is gone just me now my sister gone back my brother gone forward too soon too fast too long. I want to wrap all the trees on my back tie all the threads of stone and rag and bone so I will not get lost. Do not hurry the starry ash mouths say. You will live. I do not know I say, I do not know if I am living or dead or nothing or something or maybe I am a giraffe a giraffe dreaming of walking dreaming of a giraffe that sings hungry and thirsty for a name a name like Abdullah who knows hunger and fire I lift my branch and toss the sun and pull down the moon and bring up the breath under my face with spotted skin with scars in the shape of cracked crystals.

Mud Drawing #25. The Village Fly

I study scalps crawl under them
under the green muscle and the red bone

The shape of a tiny cloud loosens into another cloud then something takes
place it is jagged it is wingless it has the face of many faces when I balance
close my eyes in each eye of the many faces they all turn back into me into
my own veins and mirrors that is when I follow them here there there
there here one two one one then three all their numbers all their names
all their things without names all their forms going to each other all their
cries and all their songs and all their hopes in all their tatters and all their
lives and all their twisted flaming embraces and all their tangled skins and
all their feet let go

I study scalps crawl under them
under the muscle green and the bone red
then I rise.

Mud Drawing #26. Abdullah, the Village Boy with One Eye

No food. No food no food no food no food!
just Ibrahim moving circles on the wall the wall the wall
just Ibrahim waving hand shapes on the wall without without the village
or the hut or the rag door or the dirt floor or the twig bed
just Ibrahim not speaking anymore or Sahel just Sahel picking up sticks
where bones bones are piled where the faces rot rot where everyone is
asleep just Sahel pasting things saying things to me I don't see Ibrahim she
says one two one
he is ahead of me somewhere but I can see him somehow I don't see Sahel
she is behind me somewhere but I can hear her somehow Sahel nothing
nothing nothing
no food no water no cows no goats no father no mother one sister one
brother

one

Television Box in the Last Village Hut

Juba, South Sudan, Africa

Inside the New Africa Series:

News Anchor Bart Crimson Interviews an Ex-Janjaweed

Confidential

Bart Crimson: Please continue, just a few minutes left
. . .

Janjaweed: Near a cave. Back on truck. Alone. He is
hiding. Heh. Gripping a bucket of water. Come out!
So I can shoot a rebel! He showed his head and asked
if I could take him to America. With his two friends
from village, heh. You crazy? America? I said with my
Kalash on his neck. Dunno he said. He was just a few
years. Heh, younger than me. Except . . .

Bart: Wait a minute. Look, aren't you both Muslim?
Helloo? And you are Arab, okeh, so . . .

Janjaweed: Stop!

Bart: Uh . . .

Janjaweed: You do not know those words.

Bart: Look . . .

Janjaweed: A machine gave you those words. Like every-
one else. In the United States eh. Ah . . .

Bart: You. Do not know *those* words, my friend.

Janjaweed: Everyone in Africa. Knows *those* words.

Bart: Look, I have a show here . . . can we get back
to the boy?

Janjaweed: Eh. Ahh. I kill many like him. Rebel African
boy, heh. Taxi! He said. You take me? I give you my
gold. He said. And he showed me necklaces, heh. You
think I am fool? Gold? Empty bullet casing. Heh. Dung!
Show me where's America! I said. Heh. Heh. America
heh. And I'll go too. Maybe I be richman there. Drive
taxi like you. I said. With Kalash on his face. And.
Heh. I'll let you. Go.

Bart: Didn't you say you shot him?

Janjaweed: Yes. Shot him. He broke on the ground. Show me America! Rebel boy! I said. Heh. Fingers bloody he scratched the dirt he jabbed his arms a little he spilled his filthy bucket spitting blood. This the way. He said. Mashing mud with his head. Up and down. Left him there. Don't know. Alive. Heh. Dead. Ahh.

The horses never ceased from galloping every bullet that shot out from their masters made them kick faster made them groan deeper made them into something that broke apart and let out a trembling suffering wave across the desert.

Mud Drawing #27. The Kalashnikov AK-47

In my language of Kalash, I spoke to them
For the first time, I said—

Help me

Take me with you
Wipe my face
I am scarred and bloody
I suffer from tempests
From implacable winds between my temples
I want to taste what you taste
Cruel breads
Stews of knees and boiling tongues
Putrid waters

I only know the young hands and
The uncertain fingers of my master

So I was born
So was my destiny

It is the mountains that I love
I call to them and I call to them
As I fall to your side
As my master sleeps

My name is Kala

Inside the New Africa Series:
News Anchor Bart Crimson Interviews an Ex-Janjaweed

Confidential

Bart Crimson: Let's move on. We are not getting any-where. You mentioned the Russian weapons. Who else provides military resources? Let's get with it, ok?
Janjaweed: Heh ahhh. China. 55 million worth between 2004 and 2006. Small arms heh. Kalash. Heh.
Bart: Mmmmm mmmmm.

Mud Drawing #28. Abdullah, the Village Boy with One Eye

No trees. No mother no father one sister one brother
I follow.

Mud Drawing #29. The Village Ant

& ticking & tapping
& carrying & knotting
& stinging & sniffing
& digging & splashing
& crapping & sniffing
& spitting & mashing
& blooding & snapping
& mashing & wrapping
& digging & wrapping

& wrapping
& stinking
& spitting
& digging
& crapping
& sniffing
& digging
& digging
& spitting

Even though others laughed at Ibrahim made stories about him and his mud drawings he did not care. To them it was all dirty black soil shooting up from all their toes. For Ibrahim it was different. If he fanned out the mud with his hands and fingers and even with his head bobbing up and down as if bowing to a distant ancestor there was a way a road a horizon that would lead him and his tiny band to freedom.

Mud Drawing #30. Abdullah, the Village Boy with One Eye

Sahel!
One sister! I say
I wait for you but you are busy busy dragging a stick school on the graves
I wait for you but you are busy busy scratching a chalkboard with flies

Sitting
  Waiting
  The clouds
  The winds

Mud Drawing #31. Ibrahim, the Village Boy

All night we hid in the cave. We had just returned from burying the dead.
Mr. America I said while I carried two plastic water buckets balanced on
a wooden branch broom across my shoulders. Janjaweed laughed with
their teeth out and their noses open. And their Kalash crackle. And their
necklaces of sacred seeds and sacred torn dried ears of prayer cloth rattling
against the Kalash. They pulled their privates and tightened their hands.
Back at the cave I made a Kalash. Out of the mud on the floor. Made
a taxi. Made mother Nasra's face appear on the wall. Listen, she said,
Freedom is a flame that rises out of your heart. Your enemies will never
kill it. If it does disappear it is because you smashed it, because you are
your own enemy. Then it will be too late, Ibrahim. Days later angry ants
chewed my ankle. Next day my leg was swollen. Ibrahim, see the ants?
They bite you because they are fighting for their life. Grandmother Um
used to say. One ant fights for all the ants. You must fight for your life too.
When you grow up you must fight for me too. For the rest of us. We are
the tiny peoples. We are the ants of Darfur, of Africa. We endure hard rains
and droughts. Even if you fight with leaves and dirt. Even if you do it with
your mud hands on the walls of the village.

So I called him when we saw them coming again. Mr. America!
Here's your gold!

Mud Drawing #32. Ibrahim, the Village Boy

This is the gold, this! I said to Abdullah.
Gold? Ibrahim?

We must look for more, Abdullah. I'll show you how we are going to melt
it.
We are going to Senegal. And this, I said, holding up the empty casing to
the moon, this is our taxi from Senegal to New York. To United States.
Abdullah smiled a little smile and whistled a tune with a casing flying over
my head. After the chores of getting water and sweeping the night soil, we
sat on the ground. Next day Abdullah laid them out and waited quietly.
And waited. Ibrahim! They are not melting! That's not gold. Shhh . . . I
pointed to a stone. We need to make them melt. We don't want bullets. We
want gold, eh? What if we pound them smash them smash them smash!
Sahel repeated. Smash them smash them! Abdullah slapped his hands on
the ground. He flew out of the cave calling out for a stone. Stone! Stone!
Sahel followed him, Stone! Near the cave where we hid I dragged a water
bucket past Abdullah and Sahel carrying water too. A hot wire stung me I
jumped on one foot and spilled my buckets hopped and limped back and
stumbled flat on my face. Eating mud I made mud with the runny brown
water I spit Stone! Stone! I said. But no stone came. Sat up and thought of
mother Nasra and my father Muhammad gone but I knew they still were
on this earth that I was still on it too so I smeared mud on my face and on
my arms and scooped it from the ground and I drew a camel-shaped taxi
that could carry all of us and I carved out a road so we could all escape and
I splattered more mud so I could dig a tunnel to Senegal so we wouldn't

get caught by the bandits and thrown into a ghost house where no one ever gets out and I knocked down little piles of Janjaweed and I drove over their watery Toyotas and pounded their tiny Kalash made of pieces of broken straw and I bounced on the coast of Senegal and sped up up up up high higher than all of us standing on each other's shoulders until I landed in New York I slowed my taxi opened the soft door stepped out Sahel too and Abdullah the waters of the ocean flushed us out of the taxi on a round street under the dark winged stone of the sun.

Television Box in the Last Village Hut
Juba, South Sudan, Africa

Inside the New Africa Series:

News Anchor Bart Crimson Interviews an Ex-Janjaweed
Confidential

Bart Crimson: Now, now, why would Russia and China support the Sudanese government and be at odds with the USA?

Janjaweed: Why would United States eh. Support South Korea and be odds with China eh ahh. Why would U.S. sell, no, ah, heh. Give billions in weapons, for free heh. To Colombia. Heh. In exchange for no negotiating oil sales with China. Heh. There's no odds, Mr. Crimson.

Bart: What do you mean huh? No odds? Explain that!

Janjaweed: Oil. Everybody love oil. Sudanese Nile crude. 480,000 barrels. Abyei South Sudan oil. New pipelines every second built in the north, Mr.Crimson. U.S. love Columbia oil. Spain love Venezuela oil. Heh ahh ahh. Russia love oil. Sudan president love oil. USA Love love! Ahh. Heh.

Bart: What about you? Ugh. Do you love oil? Come on!

Janjaweed: We. Janjaweed. Just drops. We get heh. That's all we get. Little ants of oil. Little flies . . . of oil. Your politician love oil. Middle East heh.

Bart: We are going to weather. Thank you! Back in a moment. Ugh!

Janjaweed: Wait, heh. Let me tell you what I. Love . . .

Mud Drawing #33. Ibrahim, the Village Boy

Abdullah?

Doesn't look like a stone. It's an Antonov bombshell from Russian war planes, I said. It fell out of the sky and blew open. Sahel clapped. Abdullah tapped his fingers on the boney metal, then he jumped, and made a drum sound boom boom boom looked at me with his one big whirly eye and sang

Stone stone fell out of the sky
Stone stone do you know why?
Stone stone do you know why?
Stone stone so you won't be alone
Stone stone Ibrahim make you gold!

Television Box in the Last Village Hut
Juba, South Sudan, Africa

Inside the New Africa Series:

News Anchor Bart Crimson Interviews an Ex-Janjaweed

Confidential

Bart Crimson: Ok, ok, it's hard to believe that you are comparing the government of the United States to the Sudanese government. As you know the president of Sudan acquired his position through a military coup in 1987. That's a long way from how the U.S. operates.
Janjaweed: That is insignificant. Oil. Is. Significant. Power. Is significant.
Bart: Ah, signi . . .
Janjaweed: China. Russia. Weapons. Significant. Janjaweed significant. Village insignificant. Dead insignificant. Except there was a limit. You understand? Heh.
Bart: Lissen, you don't expect . . . ahhh . . . the American and European public—as you know, there's millions of viewers watching this segment—you don't expect that the global audience is going to believe you quit being a Janjaweed because you had a little dream? Do you? Come on buddy! Get with it!
Janjaweed: Heh. You expect too many things.
Bart: Ohhh . . . come on!
Janjaweed: Africa expect nothing. Food. Water. Two things. Only two. Maybe three. Power. Ahh heh but let me tell you what I love.

Mud Drawing #34. Ibrahim, the Village Boy

After taking turns pounding and flattening the bullet casings with a jagged
bomb piece on top of a fatter bomb piece of the bomb, we laid out the
gold. Scratchy strips and faceless coins. Some in the shape of tears. Others,
sharp bird beaks. Sahel put the bird beak in her ear—
Kriii kriiii, she said. Kriii, kriiiiii!
Pounded one more bullet casing the size of three fingers. We all poked
holes into each piece and with an old string Sahel and Abdullah threaded
them into a necklace.

Each gold piece a taxi! I said. This one!
And that one! And that one! Abdullah said, then dancing silly, he sang—

Stone stone
    fell out of the sky
        Stone stone do you know why?
   Stone stone
               do you know why?
        Stone stone so you won't be alone
         Stone stone Ibrahim make you gold!

Abdullah kept repeating things. After a while he stopped talking and singing like he used to. After a while his words were little Antonovs the shrieks the bullets those things slipping out of the sky the earth the night and the day. After a while Abdullah just mumbled and stuttered. How could a singer never sing again? Ibrahim said.

Television Box in the Last Village Hut

Juba, South Sudan, Africa

Inside the New Africa Series:

News Anchor Bart Crimson Interviews an Ex-Janjaweed

Confidential

Bart Crimson: Look amigo. You killed thousands. So.
Let's stop the politico crap. And the psychologistics
on dreams ok? Believe me there is no one on the planet
that is going to buy that, aha. Okeh.

Janjaweed: Kill kill kill. You kill kill kill. We kill
kill kill. Heh.

Bart: Wait a minute buddy. This is not about us. Ok?
This is about you! And your dirty little comrades. Got
it? Ugh. Ahh. Ugh.

Janjaweed: U.S. like talk. Social issue talk. Television
talk. Radio talk show. Africa no talk.

Bart: Look, buddy. We're running out of time . . . we
. . .

Janjaweed: No pillows. No water. Sudan just oil. One
thing. Oil. And orders. Two things. Oil and orders.
Like you maybe. Not social issue. No talk. Ahh.

Mud Drawing #35. Abdullah, the Village Boy with One Eye

No food. One sister no food one sister no food no food.
Just run. Sahel! Run ruuuuuuuuuun!

Mud Drawing #36. Ibrahim, the Village Boy

From my cave. Mr. America! I called in a stand-up voice. Not a kicked
down to the ground voice. Mr. America! Sahel and Abdullah behind me.
The rebel ant! Fly! Mr. America said with his mouth stretched up crooked.
Here's your gold!
Slipped off the necklace from my neck. It's from my mother Nasra, I said.
Made out of little pieces of gold.
Mr. America was without words. For blessings, I said. For victory!
Shut up ant! Mr. America said. Have more? His guard asked.
Yes.
If you let me go, and my brother and sister too. Sahel let out a whimper.
Mr. America hung the casings over his neck. Stood up in the back of his
truck. Raised his Kalash. With both hands over his head. Then aimed it at
me. But the Kalash coughed and stuttered. Mr. America howled some-
thing at the sky and they sped out.

We escaped.
Well. I guess this is where I drop you off, Ms. I'll get your luggage.

They did not cradle a Kalashnikov AK-47. They ran. They day-prayed and starved night after night. They were no match for the Janjaweed. Ibrahim stopped Abdullah and Sahel and told them—Inside the Janjaweed all the blood of the dead will eat him. This is the way it shall be. This is what our grandmother Um told me.

Television Box in the Last Village Hut
Juba, South Sudan, Africa

Inside the New Africa Series:
News Anchor Bart Crimson Interviews an Ex-Janjaweed
Confidential

Bart Crimson: All right, all right. Look. You don't want to answer my questions. Ok. We can just go around and around in circles here. Why didn't you just join the Sudanese Liberation Army? You sound like you've gone AWOL from the Janjaweed. You might as well take off the mask. You are definitely confused. Maybe you need a psychiatrist. Why did you leave the Janjaweed? Is this killing ever going to stop? Period! You have thirty seconds.

Janjaweed: I am not who I was. I am not that man anymore. I loved to ride the night with my Kalash. Await power and death and killing crawling up my arms. Then come back alive filled with it. I am not that man now.

Bart: Can you do me a favor? Answer the question Mr. Janjaweed, ok buddy. Or ex-Janjaweed. Whatever you are. I am not believing you here. Come on! Fifteen seconds.

Janjaweed: The rebel boy was alive, the ant. I know when they are dead. Heh. I know when they will die. I know how they die. My Kalash knows. But ah, I don't know when they are alive. His face was buried in the mud.

Mud Drawing #37. The Village Ant

Wake up!

Wakeupwakeupwakeupwakeupwakeup!

Mud Drawing #38. Abdullah, the Village Boy with One Eye

One one one one
One one one one one one one one one one   one
One one
One one one one one one one one one one one one one one one one one
one one one one one   one one one one one
one one one one one   one one one one one
One one one one one one one one one one one one one one one one
One one one one one one one   one one
One one
        One one one one
One one one one one one one one   one one
One one one one one one one one one one one one one one one one one
One one one one one one one one one one one one one one one one one
One
One one one one one one one one one one one one one one one one one
One
One one one one one one one one one one one one one one one one one
One
                                 One

Abdullah! Abdullah! Sahel said. See the new sun? Above you? The many suns? One for me. One for you, one for Ibrahim. One for me!

From the cave into the darkness. The three did not know if they would get out. They would not survive. There was wire. There were guards and weapons. There were ghost houses where they would bind you in secret and beat you until your human face would melt off. This was the Sahel. Below the treacherous belt of the Sahara. The region of mirages and storms.

Inside the New Africa Series:

News Anchor Bart Crimson Interviews an Ex-Janjaweed

Confidential

Janjaweed: The death inside your life. That. That heh. Is the limit. The rest. Insignificant. Not significant.
Bart: Well, yeah. Ok, ok. Right, well, ok, ladies and gentlemen, that's it for *Inside the New Africa Series—a Special on the New Sudan.* Ugh. Wait! What are you doing, buddy? Why are you taking off your mask?

Mud Drawing #39. Ibrahim, the Village Boy

Sahel and Abdullah were silent. Starved. Taxi! I called out. Come! Taxi to Senegal! Abdullah stared dreamily at me with a swollen blue face. Swollen from an insect bite. Swollen from everything. Come Abdullah! Let's go. Janjaweed gone! Come. Taxi is waiting! Abdullah limped. Said nothing. Abdullah floated his hands over my shoulders like when we played games in the village. His head looked up over me. He was almost asleep. Sahel came up behind him. Placed her little hands on his hips. She made a sickly honking sound. Some leaves roared past us. We followed them. Out

Ghost House Run

it was almost as if the ancestor spirits or mountains or the unnamable thousands were calling them back to Sudan or urging them forward—but they did not turn back bullets came to them and broke their flight they fell to the sands and were dragged away by the shrouded men mumbling and laughing and catching their breath and spitting and letting it come down their long bone sun scorched faces the tiny tilted filthy shack pestilent shack was waiting for them as it had waited for all those hunted ones that dared to outsmart the Sahel to evade the Janjaweed en route to something they had never seen something without blood and fire sliding out of its eyes and rape and torn innards and chopped faces and raped again sisters mothers child woman flesh—then

it closed its doors and locked them—Ibrahim Sahel Abdullah—gape-
mouth men stood and hunched in front of them and sneered and poked
them with their beloved Kalash hand-oiled

Sahel turned her watery bitten face toward Ibrahim's stutter breath the Kalash long beat Ibrahim the wounds and welts fruited on his face in that dark that was infinite

Abdullah fell into dry sharp howls the blood spilled and spotted redblackness on the walls of blueblackness the Kalash man loosened his mouth and pushed out his teeth like the Kalash pulled its nose out one then two then three Kalash men snorted and drank and smoked and spit and jerked up and jerked out of the shining dark shooting while one the one with one eye lay still on the dripping floor just one one alone forever in the cuts of laughter and cries Sahel stood up somehow she stood up and ended her sobbing and wheezing and coughing gulping from the mucous sliding down her throat her rag shirt half-ripped by the men with the Kalash she stood up alone in the room of man-evils as if she had wings and a sky where she could ascend and breathe for the first time

Juba

New Capital of South Sudan, Africa, 2011

Television Box in the Last Village Hut
Juba, South Sudan, Africa

Inside the New Africa Series:

News Anchor Bart Crimson Interviews an Ex-Janjaweed
Confidential

Bart Crimson: What do you think you are doing? Hey! The program is over Mr.

Janjaweed: Not significant. Your program . . . buddy!

Bart: Hey, wait a minute. What? You! Wait I said. You, you! You are no Janjaweed!

Janjaweed: My name is Abdullah. No it isn't.

Bart: What kinda sham is this? You know this is going to cause you some problems. Look, the whole show is in jeopardy. We need this. The new Sudan. South Sudan. Everything. What are you?

Janjaweed: Words. Words? Not significant now. Wor . . .

Bart: Hey! Hey! Someone get the producer right now! Call security!

i wake up

little girl makes toilet behind me
at the cemetery of forgotten stones
in our park of bones where we sleep
raise my head above
                                floating branches
            flying roots
            Kalashnikoved out   from the earth
people chant Juba! Juba!
Our new Capital!
            with my long leg and
long foot down below
i scratch *C A P I T   A L*
inside the cut belly of
                                an empty green bowl

wake upwake up
hold the child's cloudy hand hurry
i say

before we leave i

listen to mother Nasra's laugh
she say eh Ibrahim you are the wild one. The one always running. Here
and there. The one that can't stand still. The one digging for gold where
there is none. The one talking to twigs thinking they are Janjaweed. The
one smearing dirty water on your face by the tree in the middle of the
village. The one rubbing mud on the walls in thick and skinny circles and
telling us they are taxis. Taxis to Senegal. Taxis that can fly into the sky.
Taxis to New York. Taxis that can pull forever. From bullets and guards.
From check-points and guns. Taxis that can burn through the land of the
dead. Eh Ibrahim?

About the Author

Juan Felipe Herrera is a noted writer, performer, poet, and playwright. He is a professor in the Department of Creative Writing at the University of California, Riverside. Herrera was educated at the University of California, Los Angeles, and Stanford University, and has an MFA from the University of Iowa Writers' Workshop. He has published twenty-eight volumes of poetry, prose, theater, children's books, and young adult novels, including *187 Reasons Mexicanos Can't Cross the Border: Undocuments 1971–2007* (2007); *Half of the World in Light: New and Selected Poems* (University of Arizona Press, 2008), which was a recipient of the PEN/Beyond Margins Award and was a winner of the National Book Critics Circle award in poetry; and *Cinnamon Girl: Letters Found Inside a Cereal Box* (2005). He is the winner of over fifty awards, fellowships, and honorable mentions, including the John Simon Guggenheim Memorial Foundation Poetry Fellowship in 2010, the PEN USA Award in Poetry, the Hungry Mind Award of Distinction, the Ezra Jack Keats Award, two Latino Hall of Fame Poetry awards, the National Book Critics Circle Award, the University of California at Berkeley Regent's Fellowship, and fellowships from the National Endowment for the Arts and the California Arts Council; he is a New York Times Notable. He was appointed California poet laureate in March 2012 and is the first Chicano writer to serve in the post.